Published by Creative Paperbacks
P.O. Box 227, Mankato, Minnesota 56002
Creative Paperbacks is an imprint of
The Creative Company
www.thecreativecompany.us

Design by The Design Lab
Production by Chelsey Luther
Art direction by Rita Marshall
Printed in the United States of America

Photographs by Alamy (All Canada Photos),
Dreamstime (Isselee, Steve Keller, Tim Martin,
Vanessagifford, Vasiliy Vishnevskiy), Getty Images
(Jim Brandenburg, David McNew, Charles Marion
Russell), iStockphoto (Eric Foltz, Conor Quinlan),
National Geographic (TOM MURPHY, JOEL
SARTORE), SuperStock (Nomad)

Library of Congress Cataloging-in-Publication Data
Bodden, Valerie.
Bison / by Valerie Bodden.
p. cm. — (Amazing animals)
Summary: A basic exploration of the appearance,
behavior, and habitat of bison, shaggy beasts of
the plains and woods. Also included is a story from
folklore explaining why bison have humps.
Includes bibliographical references and index.
ISBN 978-1-60818-085-1 (hardcover)
ISBN 978-0-89812-787-4 (pbk)
1. Bison—Juvenile literature. I. Title.
QL737.U53B63 2013
599.64'3—dc23   2011050263

First Edition
9 8 7 6 5 4 3 2 1

AMAZING ANIMALS

BISON

BY VALERIE BODDEN

CREATIVE
PAPERBACKS

Only about 1,000 adult wisent live in the wild today

Bison are big animals related to cows. There are two **species** of bison. The American bison lives in the United States and Canada. It is the largest land animal in North America. The wisent (*VEE-zunt*) lives on the **continent** of Europe (*YOO-rup*).

continent one of Earth's seven big pieces of land

species kinds of animals that look alike and can have young together

A bison's body is covered with thick brown or black fur. Both male and female bison have horns on their heads. American bison have a big hump on their shoulders.

A male bison's head has more of a triangle shape than a female's

American bison can weigh more than 2,000 pounds (907 kg)! They are about 6.5 feet (2 m) tall. Wisent usually have longer legs than American bison. All bison can run up to 35 miles (56 km) per hour over a short space.

Running bison make a loud noise that sounds like thunder

Plains and wood bison are the two kinds of American bison

Most American bison live in western North America. Some live in forests. Others live on **plains**. The wisent lives in woods in parts of eastern Europe.

plains large, flat areas of land with few trees

A bison's main food is grass. Sometimes bison eat twigs or bark, too. In the winter, bison use their big heads to push snow off the grass.

When animals feed on grass, it is called "grazing"

A female bison gives birth to one baby at a time. The baby is called a calf. The calf can run a few hours after it is born. It has to watch out for wolves and bears. Bison can live 25 years in the wild.

Bison calves are generally born in April and May

Herds of bison walk together to find food

Bison live in **bands** of 20 to 60 animals. Sometimes many bands come together to make a herd. A herd might have hundreds or thousands of bison.

bands groups of animals

BISON

16

Bison like to roll in dirt holes called wallows. The dirt helps them cool off. It also keeps their skin safe from bug bites. If bison get scared, they might stampede, or run as fast as they can.

*Bison roll around in dirt
that is dry or muddy*

There were once millions of American bison. But people killed almost all of them. Today, the biggest group of wild bison lives in Yellowstone National Park. Some people go there to see them. Others see bison at zoos. It is fun to watch these shaggy animals eat, sleep, and wallow!

People called American Indians hunted bison for food

A *Bison Story*

Why do bison have humps? **American Indians** used to tell a story about this. They said that a bison father told his calf to stay out of the brown grass where the birds lived. But the calf went into the brown grass. This made the creator mad. He put a stick on the calf's shoulders. Soon a big hump grew in that spot. From then on, all bison had humps!

American Indians the first people to live in North America before white people came

Read More

Frisch, Aaron. *Prairies*. Mankato, Minn.: Creative Education, 2008.

George, Jean Craighead. *The Buffalo Are Back*. New York: Dutton Children's Books, 2010.

Wrobel, Scott. *Bison*. North Mankato, Minn.: Smart Apple Media, 2001.

Web Sites

Enchanted Learning: Bison
http://www.enchantedlearning.com/subjects/mammals/bison/Bisoncoloring.shtml
This site has a picture of a bison to print and color.

National Geographic Kids Creature Features: American Bison
http://kids.nationalgeographic.com/kids/animals/creaturefeature/american-bison/
This site has bison facts, pictures, and videos.

Index